HIGH
HOPES

HIGH HOPES

A PHOTOBIOGRAPHY OF
JOHN F. KENNEDY

BY DEBORAH HEILIGMAN

NATIONAL GEOGRAPHIC

WASHINGTON, D.C.

John M. Fahey, Jr., *President and Chief Executive Officer*

Gilbert M. Grosvenor, *Chairman of the Board*

Nina D. Hoffman, *Executive Vice President, President of Books and Education Publishing Group*

Ericka Markman, *Senior Vice President, President of Children's Books and Education Publishing Group*

STAFF FOR THIS BOOK

Nancy Laties Feresten, *Vice President, Editor-in-Chief of Children's Books*

Suzanne Patrick Fonda, *Project Editor*

Bea Jackson, *Art Director, Children's Books*

Susan Blair, *Illustrations Editor*

Marty Ittner, *Designer*

Carl Mehler, *Director of Maps*

Joseph F. Ochlak, *Map Research*

Gregory Ugiansky, *Map Production*

Mark Wentling, *Indexer*

R. Gary Colbert, *Production Director*

Lewis R. Bassford, *Production Manager*

Vincent P. Ryan, *Manufacturing Manager*

The body text of the book is set in Trump Mediaeval. The display text is set in Waters Titling.

LIBRARY OF CONGRESS
CATALOGING-IN-PUBLICATION DATA
Heiligman, Deborah.
High Hopes: A Photobiography of John F. Kennedy / by Deborah Heiligman.
p. cm.
Summary: Photographs and text trace the life of President John F. Kennedy.
ISBN 0-7922-6141-0
1. Kennedy, John F. (John Fitzgerald), 1917–1963—Pictorial works—Juvenile literature. 2. Presidents—United States—Pictorial works—Juvenile literature. 3. Presidents—United States—Biography—Juvenile literature. [1. Kennedy, John F. (John Fitzgerald), 1917–1963. 2. Presidents.] I. Title.
E842.Z9H45 2003   973.922'092—dc21   2003007819

Printed in the United States of America

FRONT COVER AND TITLE PAGE: **On a trip to Mexico in 1962, crowds greet President Kennedy with cheers, confetti, and flowers.**

OPPOSITE: **President Kennedy and the First Lady (his wife, Jackie) greet guests at an Inaugural Ball.**

ACKNOWLEDGMENTS

The author would like to thank Melody Miller, Senior Aide to Senator Edward Kennedy and longtime spokesperson for the Kennedy family, for reading the manuscript, and Allan Goodrich and James B. Hill in the Audiovisual Library at the John F. Kennedy Library for their assistance.

Thank you to Aaron Weiner and Benjamin Weiner for research help, and to Jonathan Weiner for moving over to make room for JFK. Thank you to Mrs. Sandberg and her fourth-grade class for answering my questions. I would like to thank the following people for sharing their memories and insights of JFK: Wendy Forman (who wrote a campaign song for JFK in high school), David Greenwald (who does a great JFK impression), Martha Hewson, Ellen Miller, Charlotte Murphy of Choate Rosemary Hall, Steve Rubin (who was a civil rights worker and President of the ACLU of Louisiana), Shira Stern, Julie Stockler, Jerome H. Weiner, Kay Winters, and the telemarketer who called when I was on deadline and did her rendition of Marilyn Monroe singing "Happy Birthday, Mr. President"—the whole song. I hope she didn't get fired. A special thank you to Susan Korman for lending me her family's JFK treasures. And one to my mother, who held me while we watched the funeral and who, in her wisdom, saved some really good stuff about JFK. I wish you were here to read this book.

NOTES ABOUT QUOTES

"High Hopes" campaign song (dust jacket and p. 29)**:** Words by Sammy Cahn, music by James Van Heusen copyright © 1959 (renewed) Maraville Music Corp. All rights reserved. Used by permission, Warner Bros. Publications U.S. Inc., Miami, FL 33014. **Display quotes:** The quotes from John F. Kennedy are taken from his speeches or public remarks. Most of the following can be found on the JFK Library Web site *(see page 63 for URL)*: p. 5 Announcement of candidacy for the Presidency, January 2, 1960: JFK Library, speeches; p. 14 Cable from Joseph to JFK: JFK Library, biography; p. 19 Public remark, JFK Library, forum page, November 11, 2002; p. 23 Speech given October 20, 1960: **www.jfklink.com/speeches/jfk/oct60/jfk201060_clancy.html;** p. 25 *The Fitzgeralds and the Kennedys,* by Doris Kearns Goodwin, p. 707; p. 26 Often quoted. Can be found in the congressional memorial tribute to Jackie: **http://www.access.gpo.gov/congress/senate/senate30.html;** p. 28 from *Profiles in Courage.* Can be found on JFK Library, popular quotations page; p. 32 Inaugural Address: JFK Library, speeches; p. 36 Inaugural Address: JFK Library, speeches; p. 40 Accepting party's nomination, July 15, 1960: JFK Library, speeches; p. 43 Address to the United Nations General Assembly, September 25, 1961: JFK Library, popular quotations page; p. 51 JFK Library, popular quotations page; p. 54 President Johnson made this statement to the press after JFK was assassinated: **www.time.com/time/daily/special/Kennedy/8.html;** p. 60 Inaugural Address. JFK Library, speeches. Back cover Address at American University, June 10, 1963, JFK Library, speeches. **Text quotes** (full bibliographic and Web site information listed on page 63): P. 12 "...I am urging you to do the best you can..." JFK Library Web site, biography of JFK. P. 14 "At 1500 you die..." Robert Dallek article, *Atlantic Monthly*, p.5. P. 15 "Living a life of leisure..." clip from "Life in Camelot" video; "When the going gets tough..." JFK Library Web site, biography of JFK. P. 19 "Ship at two o'clock!" Ballard, p.88. P. 20 "seems to have cut into the natural order of things..." Goodwin, p. 699. P. 21 "I got Jack into politics" *McCalls,* August 1947. P. 26 "I knew right away..." Goodwin, p. 770; "a darling child" JFK Library Web site, biography of Jacqueline Bouvier Kennedy; "I married a whirlwind." clip from "Life in Camelot" video. P. 31 "I had never seen him looking so fit." Museum of Broadcast Communications Web site. P. 34 "terrific" *LIFE,* November 21, 1960, p.36. P. 35 "Good Morning," oft told, as in speech by Senator Edward Kennedy August 15, 2000, **abcnews.go.com;** "Of all the millions..." "John Fitzgerald Kennedy," Readers Digest video, vol. 2; "Men and women will be..." JFK Library Web site, speeches page. PP. 38–39 "He's not doing anything." *Redbook,* June, 1961, p. 72. P. 41 Hamster quotes, *Redbook,* p. 76; "There is an old saying..." Salinger, pp. 42–43. P. 42 "the man who accompanied" oft quoted, as in "John Fitzgerald Kennedy," Readers Digest video, vol. 3. P. 43 "I'd rather shake hands..." "John Fitzgerald Kennedy," Readers Digest video, vol. 3. "We can't let that happen." Reeves, p. 170. P. 44 "Ich bin ein..." Remarks at the Rudolph Wilde Platz June 26, 1963, JFK Library Web site, speeches. P. 48 All quotes from speech at American University June 10, 1963, JFK Library Web site, speeches. P. 52: "I kept thinking..." Jackie Kennedy's testimony to the Warren Commission. P. 55: "In Dallas Texas..." *TV Guide,* January 25, 1964, p.23; "The President died" "Walter Cronkite Remembers" video; "He's been shot!" *TV Guide,* p. 33. P. 61 "the world's most valuable resource..." UNICEF Appeal July 25, 1963, JFK Library, popular quotations. P. 62 "landing a man on the moon" Special message to Congress May 25, 1961, JFK Library, speeches.

"I HAVE DEVELOPED AN IMAGE OF AMERICA
AS FULFILLING A NOBLE AND HISTORIC ROLE AS THE
DEFENDER OF FREEDOM IN A TIME OF MAXIMUM PERIL—
AND OF THE AMERICAN PEOPLE
AS CONFIDENT, COURAGEOUS AND PERSEVERING."

The athletic Kennedy family loved to play touch football at their summer compound in Hyannis Port. Here, Jack throws the football toward Eunice (far left), Jackie, and Teddy. Bobby's wife, Ethel, is behind Jack.

FOREWORD

Like many boys and girls, I grew up in a family that was full of action. Although my family was big—there were nine children—I think we had the same experiences that most young people have: We had fun; we competed against each other; we helped each other; and we made up exciting games. We even had a squabble or two, but we also laughed a lot. Not every day was a good day, but we were taught to stick up for one another and make the best of everything.

But one thing was different: One of the children was to become President of the United States, John F. Kennedy! Jack, as we called him, was just a brother to us, but years later, he would become someone who would be known all over the United States. To us, he was smart, funny, warm, helpful, and a great competitor. To the world, he would become all that and more—a man who led our country in issues such as peace, freedom, and civil rights.

I think if he were writing this foreword today, he would not write about himself. Instead, he would write about the boys and girls of today. He would be thinking about all the wonderful things each of you can do to make the world better. He would tell each of you to look around your family, your neighborhood, your country, and try to help make it better. He would challenge you not to wait till you are old, but to help now—today! He would make you laugh and think and work hard, all at the same time. He would tell you that each person is special, no matter their religion or their race or their disability.

John F. Kennedy was a wonderful brother to me and a wonderful son to my parents. To our country, he was a wonderful President. To the world, he was strong and inspiring. When you read this book, I hope you will think of him as a man who, if he met you, would believe that you are capable of doing great things for your country. That was his magic: He believed in the goodness of people. The greatest tribute we can pay to him is to believe in each other and dedicate ourselves to doing whatever we can to make our world a little better.

Eunice Kennedy Shriver

John Fitzgerald Kennedy was not supposed to be President of the United States. His older brother, Joseph Jr., was. Joe was the "golden boy" of the Kennedy family. He was smart, handsome, strong, and healthy. He was a good student and a "good boy."

Jack, as John was called, was two years younger than Joe. He was sick a lot. He spent much of his childhood in bed, reading. Jack was not such a "good boy." He was charming and funny—and messy, late, naughty, and a so-so student.

But growing up in the wealthy, talented, and ambitious Kennedy family prepared Jack for a promising future. Joseph and Rose Kennedy gave all of their children a very strong message: You have been blessed with good fortune, so you must give back. You must make a contribution to the world.

When he was born, Jack's mother wrote on a note card:

JOHN FITZGERALD KENNEDY
BORN BROOKLINE, MASS. (83 BEALS STREET) MAY 29, 1917

Rose Fitzgerald Kennedy kept note cards on all of her nine children: Joseph Jr., John, Rosemary, Kathleen, Eunice, Patricia, Robert, Jean, and Edward. She recorded their doctor visits, shots, shoe sizes, and illnesses. She had a lot of illnesses to write down for Jack. When he was not quite three he became very sick with scarlet fever and almost died. His father and mother were terrified. This was for Jack the beginning of a life filled with illness and pain. He had bronchitis, chicken pox, ear infections, German measles, mumps, and whooping cough. The family joke was that

Jack's closest friend and rival was his older brother, Joe Jr. Here Jack (far right) is eight and Joe ten. Perhaps it was this rivalry that made Jack the strong and successful person he became.

The house at 83 Beals Street in Brookline, Massachusetts, where John F. Kennedy was born, is now a national historic site. The family later moved to a bigger house and eventually to New York. Because they were wealthy, there were always cooks, nannies, maids, and tutors in the Kennedy home.

if a mosquito bit Jack, the mosquito would die from drinking Jack's blood. Yet Jack was a Kennedy. And Kennedys were strong. And determined.

Jack's parents came from powerful families. Joseph's father, Patrick Kennedy, was a Massachusetts state senator and a Boston political leader. Rose's father, John F. Fitzgerald, or "Honey Fitz," was a popular mayor of Boston. He served in the state senate and the U.S. House of Representatives.

Jack's father was also powerful. As a young man Joseph had set a life goal to be rich, successful, and influential. And he succeeded. He became a millionaire by the time he was 30. Joseph was not liked by everyone, mostly because of the way he used his money to get things done—including buying favors for his children. One of the reasons he was so determined to succeed was because of his religion. Joseph and Rose were both Irish Catholics. At the time, there was a lot of prejudice against Irish Catholics in Boston and around the United States. He wanted to prove that Irish Catholics were just as good as anybody else—or better.

Rose loved politics and had enjoyed campaigning with her father before she married Joseph Kennedy. But she was happy to run the house and take care of the children while Joseph went out and made money.

In 1927 the Kennedy family moved to New York, where Joseph thought there would be less prejudice against Catholics. They spent summers in Hyannis Port on Cape Cod in Massachusetts. There the Kennedy children swam, sailed, and played football. They were a close bunch, noisy and athletic. Yet Jack was often lonely because he was sick a great deal of the time and because his parents focused so much on Joe Jr. They had high hopes that Joe would grow up to be the first Catholic to be elected President of the United States.

The younger Kennedy brothers and sisters imitated everything Joe Jr. did. They admired him, but they adored Jack. Little Bobby used to wait each afternoon for Jack to come home from school, hoping they would take a walk. In those walks, Jack would tell Bobby stories of heroes and adventures from books he'd read. Jack felt good that he had someone who looked up to him.

Jack had mixed

Jack always loved summers on Cape Cod (above, top). Here he stands between his sisters Rosemary (far left) and Eunice, with Joe Jr. and Kathleen on the right. Even though he was a sickly child, Jack was determined to play sports. He made the Dexter School football team (sitting on the ground, second from right). Joe Jr. is on the bench, fourth from the left.

feelings about his big brother. He did admire Joe and was very close to him. Yet he spent most of his childhood, when he wasn't sick, trying to beat Joe—at something. He never did, not at football, or racing, or school-work, or anything else.

Their father always said they should play to win. Jack kept trying.

One day Joe and Jack had a bicycle race. They smashed into each other head-on. Joe wasn't hurt; Jack had to have 28 stitches.

Even though Joseph favored Joe Jr., Jack always felt that his father treated him fairly. But his mother was often angry at him. She felt he was too messy and late and not religious enough. One Good Friday at church she told her children to pray for a happy death. Jack said he would rather pray for two dogs. His mother was not amused.

Jack loved it when his mother read to him, and he really wished he had more of her attention. But Rose had to devote most of her attention to Rosemary, who had mental retardation, and to the younger children.

As teenagers, Joe Jr. and Jack went off to Choate, a private boarding school in Connecticut. Joe was a star football player and a star in schoolwork, too. Jack was not a great student, nor was he an award-winning athlete like his brother. But he worked on the yearbook, and he played football, basketball, and golf. And he had a lot of friends. One of those friends, LeMoyne (Lem) Billings, became a best friend for life.

Jack had a great sense of humor. He formed the Muckers Club with Lem and some other friends. Its sole purpose was to make mischief! One day the headmaster was so furious at Jack about something the Muckers Club did that he wanted to expel him. Jack's father talked him out of it, but he did tell his son to behave.

Joseph seemed to get a kick out of Jack's antics. After all, Joe Jr. was the one who was going to be President; Jack was allowed to have fun. But Joseph did encourage Jack to work harder. In a letter he wrote: "...I am urging you to do the best you can. I am not expecting too much, and I will not be disappointed if you don't turn out to be a real genius, but I think you can be a really worthwhile citizen with good judgment and understanding."

It helped Jack that Joseph put his ambitions on Joe Jr. It meant Jack could be himself and not worry about his future.

In fact, Jack was not sure he would even have a future. He was very, very sick during his teenage years. He was in and out of hospitals with terrible stomach pains and digestive problems. The doctors had trouble figuring out what was wrong and how to help him. Jack was miserable and scared. Still he kept his sense of humor.

A Plea for a raise
by Jack Kennedy
Dedicated to my
Mr. J. P. Kennedy

Chapter I
My recent allowance
is 40¢. This I used for aeroplanes
and other playthings of childhood but now I am a scout
and I put away my childish
things. Before I would spend
20¢ of my ¢.. allowance
and in five minutes I
would have empty pockets
and nothing to gain and
20¢ to lose. When I a
a scout I have to buy

canteens, haversacks, blankets
searchlidgs poncho things
that will last for years
and I can always use it
while I can use a
cholcolate marshmellow
sunday with vanilla ice
cream and so I put in
my plea for a raise of
thirty cents for me to buy
scout things and pay my
own way more around.
Finis

John Fitzgerald Francis
Kennedy

Even though Joseph was a strict and demanding father, that didn't stop Jack from standing up to him when he wanted something. In this letter, written when he was about 12, he asks his father for a raise in his allowance to buy Boy Scout supplies. Notice that he signed it using his confirmation name, Francis, throwing the weight of the Catholic Church into his argument! There is no evidence that he got the raise. He is 9 in the picture.

> "TWO THINGS I ALWAYS KNEW ABOUT YOU.
> ONE THAT YOU ARE SMART.
> TWO THAT YOU ARE A SWELL GUY.
> LOVE, DAD"
>
> —JOSEPH KENNEDY, SR.

At one point doctors thought he had leukemia and that he would soon die. He wrote to Lem that his white blood count was down to 3,500. "At 1500 you die. They call me '2000 to go Kennedy.'"

Doctors gave Jack a new kind of medicine—corticosteroids—to help his stomach. While the steroids helped him with some of his stomach problems, they caused bone loss in his vertebrae. This weakened his back and gave Jack terrible back pain his whole life.

His senior year at Choate Jack was voted "most likely to succeed." The boys at Choate recognized him as a leader—"Mucker" though he was—and saw a future for him that no one else saw.

After high school, Jack went to London, England, to study but was too sick to stay. Trying to break with family tradition, he enrolled at Princeton University instead of at Harvard as his father and older brother had. But he became so sick that he had to take a year off to get better. The next year he went to Harvard. Once again, he was in Joe's shadow.

In 1937, Joseph was appointed United States Ambassador to Great Britain. The whole family moved to London, except for Joe and Jack, who were in college. In the summer of 1938, Jack visited his parents and toured Europe. He became very interested in European politics and world history. That trip changed Jack's attitude about schoolwork—finally. By the time he returned to Harvard, he was determined to learn more about history, government, and current events. He majored in government and international relations. Then, in September 1939, Germany invaded Poland, and World War II began. Jack wrote his senior thesis on why England was slow to stop Hitler's aggression. He worked harder on it than on anything ever before. He graduated from Harvard with honors.

His father was so proud of his son's thesis that in 1940 he had it published as a book called *Why England Slept.* The book was well received and became a best-seller, in part because Joseph bought tens of thousands of copies. Joseph and Rose had often thought Jack could grow up to be a writer. And now it seemed his most likely path.

In fact, Jack could have lived a life of leisure because of his father's wealth. But when asked why he would work when he didn't have to, Jack answered, "Living a life of leisure is the hardest work of all." He knew he was meant to do something useful and important in the world.

He wasn't sure what career he would choose. But he did know he wanted to join the armed services. Although the United States wasn't actively involved in World War II

Jack and Lem Billings (above, right) became friends for life. They took a trip to Europe when they were in high school. Here, at The Hague, they play with a dog named Dunker.

yet, it looked certain that it would be soon. Jack tried to enlist in the Army, but because of his bad back, the Army wouldn't take him.

No bad back was going to stop him. After all, he was a Kennedy. As his father often said, "When the going gets tough, the tough get going." Jack worked hard to strengthen his back by doing exercises. A friend of his father's helped him hide his medical records, so he was able to enlist in the Navy. At first he just did paperwork. But then the Japanese attacked the U.S. Naval Base at Pearl Harbor in Hawaii on December 7, 1941, and the United States officially entered the war. Jack was determined to fight.

The close-knit Kennedy family celebrates the Fourth of July, 1938, together in England. Jack stands between Eunice (far left) and Rosemary, followed left to right by Jean, Joseph, Teddy, Rose, Joe Jr., Patricia, Bobby, and Kathleen.

Jack (far right) and some of his crew pose on PT 109 about a month before it was rammed by a Japanese destroyer. Many of the crew remained Jack's friends and staunchest supporters for the rest of his life. His courage in the time of crisis overwhelmed them.

He went to Naval Officers Training School and to the Motor Torpedo Boat Squadron Training Center. He was promoted to lieutenant, junior grade, and assigned to a U.S. base on Tulagi Island in the Solomon Islands. The U.S. and Japan were fighting over control of the Pacific. The Solomon Islands were in the middle of that struggle. In spite of his health problems, Jack wanted to be where the action was.

Twenty-five-year-old Jack was given the command of a patrol torpedo boat—PT 109. The job of PT boats was to intercept Japanese destroyers and barges carrying supplies to their bases at night. During the day the men stayed on the U.S. base. If the boats needed to be cleaned or repaired, the men did that. But most of the time they just relaxed and played poker. Jack was not a poker player. He read under a mosquito net and entertained his mates with interesting things he had read. The crews saw very little action—until August 1, 1943.

That night the commanders heard rumors that the Japanese were going to be gunning for PTs. PT 109 was one of the extra boats ordered out on patrol.

It was a moonless night in the Solomon Islands. By midnight, the crew of the PT 109 felt as if they were alone, floating in the darkness. They could not see or hear anything except static on their radio.

All of a sudden, one of Jack's men saw a big black shape racing toward their boat. "Ship at two o'clock!" he shouted. It was the Japanese destroyer *Amagiri*—378 feet long and about 50 feet wide. The 80-foot-long PT boat didn't have a chance. The *Amagiri* rammed into PT 109, splitting it in two. Two men were killed instantly. Jack was thrown down, hard, on his already painful back.

It was terrifying, with fires blazing all around. Calling out to each other, the men discovered that 11 of the original 13 were alive. Two were seriously injured and wanted to die, but Jack wouldn't let them give up.

As they clung to the wreckage, the men talked over their options. They decided to swim to Plum Pudding. It was not the closest island, but it was so small that it was the least likely to have any Japanese soldiers. In early afternoon they set out. Pappy MacMahon was in such misery from severe burns he couldn't swim. So Jack took Pappy's life jacket strap in his teeth and towed Pappy the three and a half miles to the island. The other nine men held on to a plank of wood and paddled and kicked for Plum Pudding. It took about five hours. Jack got there first. He was so exhausted and in such pain that Pappy had to help *him* onto the island.

Jack and his men spent the next week swimming to different islands, trying to find food to eat and people to rescue them. Since Pappy still couldn't swim, Jack towed him each time. At night, Jack even went out alone in shark-infested waters to try to hail an American vessel on patrol. But none came by.

Finally Jack and some others met up with two natives on Naru Island. Using his knife, Jack scratched a message on a coconut and, giving it to the natives, asked them to get help. At midnight on August 8, a week after

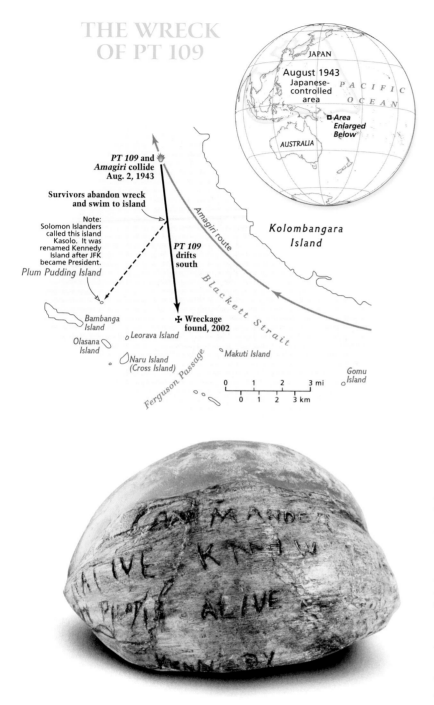

JAPAN

August 1943
Japanese-
controlled
area

PACIFIC
OCEAN

☐ *Area
Enlarged
Below*

AUSTRALIA

PT 109 and
Amagiri collide
Aug. 2, 1943

Survivors abandon wreck
and swim to island

Note:
Solomon Islanders
called this island
Kasolo. It was
renamed Kennedy
Island after JFK
became President.

Plum Pudding Island

Amagiri route

*Kolombangara
Island*

PT 109
drifts
south

Blackett Strait

*Bambanga
Island*

*Olasana
Island*

✣ Wreckage
found, 2002

○ *Leorava Island*

○ *Naru Island
(Cross Island)*

○ *Makuti Island*

Ferguson Passage

○ *Gomu
Island*

0	1	2	3 mi
0	1	2	3 km

This is the coconut that Jack carved the message on. It says: "NAURO [Naru] ISL NATIVE KNOWS POSIT HE CAN PILOT 11 ALIVE NEED SMALL BOAT KENNEDY." President Kennedy kept the coconut on his desk in the Oval Office.

the collision, the survivors of PT 109 were rescued. No one had thought they were alive. Back at the U.S. base, they were greeted as heroes.

Jack's big brother, Joe, who was a fighter pilot in Europe, heard about Jack's heroism. In 1944, almost exactly a year after Jack's PT 109 incident, Joe volunteered for a special project called Operation Aphrodite (also known as Project Anvil). In this dangerous mission, a pilot flew a plane loaded with bombs partway to a target. After the pilot and copilot parachuted out, the plane was flown by radio control until it blew up its target. On August 12, 1944, Joe Jr. never had the chance to parachute out. His plane exploded shortly after takeoff. He and his copilot were killed instantly. The Kennedy family had lost their golden boy. Jack had lost his best friend—and rival.

To honor his brother, Jack put together a book called *As We Remember Joe.* Joe's death "seems to have cut into the natural order of things," he wrote. Jack had lost the one person he could hide behind. As long as Joe was there, Jack could do what he wanted. He didn't have to answer to his father's ambitions. What now?

Joseph and Rose were devastated by Joe's death. Joseph, heartbroken, never got over the loss of Joe and could not bear to speak of him. The son he had placed his hopes on was gone forever.

But finally, he turned to Jack.

Joseph later confessed, "I got Jack into politics. I was the one. I told him Joe was dead and that it was therefore his responsibility to run for Congress. He didn't want to....But I told him he had to."

Jack said it was like being drafted into the Army. He couldn't say no.

So in 1946, Jack ran for Congress in his home state of Massachusetts. If he won, he would represent a poor district—the same district that his grandfather Honey Fitz had represented some 50 years before. His whole family helped him campaign. Joseph was his coach. After each speech, Joseph would tell him everything he did right—and wrong.

Jack received the Navy and Marine Corps Medal for his heroic rescue of the crew of PT 109 as well as the Purple Heart medal (above) for injuries he received in World War II.

Jack did not find it easy to talk to strangers on the street while campaigning. Joseph feared this would hurt his son's chances of getting elected, but it actually helped Jack. People saw him as a real and dignified person, not pushy or fake like a lot of other politicians. They responded to his charm, his wonderful smile, his humor, and his intelligence.

In 1946, Jack won his first campaign. He served in the U.S. House of Representatives for three two-year terms.

Jack had grown up with more than he needed, but he felt a very strong obligation to help people. He felt that government must provide excellent schools for all children, medical care for all people—especially poor and old people—and housing for low- and middle-income families. Rose Kennedy believed that having a sister who had trouble doing even little things instilled in all her children a compassion for those who struggled.

At the same time, Jack had a struggle of his own.

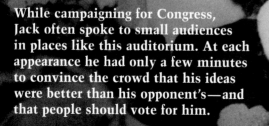

MORE JOBS•MORE HOUSING•MORE IN

JOHN F. **KENNED**

•*For* CONGRESS• **//**TH DISTRICT

While campaigning for Congress, Jack often spoke to small audiences in places like this auditorium. At each appearance he had only a few minutes to convince the crowd that his ideas were better than his opponent's—and that people should vote for him.

"POLITICAL ACTION IS THE HIGHEST
RESPONSIBILITY OF A CITIZEN."

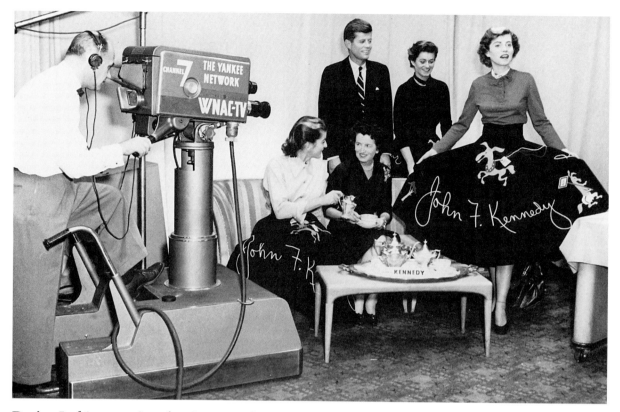

During Jack's campaigns for Congress, his sisters threw "coffees" and "teas" in constituents' homes. Jack would charm the guests by making a short speech and answering questions. From these parties he got votes and volunteers. In this televised event, sister Pat chats with Rose while Eunice, standing in front of Jack and Jean, models an autographed skirt for the camera.

During his first term in Congress he was diagnosed with Addison's disease. This disease prevents the body from producing enough adrenaline, a hormone that helps give the body energy. Untreated, it can be fatal. Doctors gave Jack more steroids, even though this medication weakened the bones in his back. As a result, his back got worse and worse.

Typical for the time, Jack did not make public how sick he was and how much medicine he had to take. He and his family did not talk about the childhood he had spent sick in bed. The pictures that were shown were of him playing football, sailing, and as a PT 109 hero. The Kennedys knew that a war hero-athlete was much more electable than someone who was in constant pain and taking a lot of medication. The Kennedy ethic was: Fight through your problems, and present the best face.

In 1948, tragedy hit the Kennedy family again. Jack's sister Kathleen (Kick) died in a plane crash. Jack was very close to her, and he was heartbroken.

"IF I WALKED OUT ON THE STAGE AND FELL FLAT ON MY FACE, FATHER WOULD SAY I FELL BETTER THAN ANYONE ELSE."

But the rest of the family rallied around him. Throughout his life he would always be surrounded by his brothers Bobby and Teddy and his sisters Eunice, Pat, and Jean. (Although by this time Rosemary had been placed in an institution to get the care she needed, she had holiday and summer visits with the family, and still does.)

It turned out that politics suited Jack. He loved working in government helping people, and he was very good at it. Sometime in his second term, he realized he didn't always have to agree with his father. Jack had different ideas from Joseph, especially about foreign policy. Unlike his father, Jack felt the United States had a responsibility to help other countries around the world and to stand up for its democratic values. Jack learned to stick by what he—not his father—believed.

After serving three terms in the House of Representatives, Jack determined he could be more influential and powerful as a U.S. senator. So, in 1952 he decided to run for the U.S. Senate. His opponent was a popular Massachusetts Republican, Henry Cabot Lodge, Jr., who was also from a powerful and wealthy political family. Lodge was not only running for reelection to the Senate, he was also managing Dwight D. Eisenhower's campaign for President. Many people did not think Jack had a chance of beating Lodge. Brother Bobby ran his campaign, and the whole family helped. Jack really listened to people and talked to them. Whether they met him in person or saw him from afar, many people felt as though he were talking directly to them and that he understood their problems. His intelligence, his caring, and his humor shone. Even though the Republican Eisenhower won the presidential election, Democrat Kennedy beat Lodge. Jack was now a senator.

Senator Kennedy was 35 and not yet married. He knew it was time to settle down and start a family. Besides, he was in love. The year before, at a dinner party, Jack had met Jacqueline Bouvier. She was a glamorous and wealthy young woman who was working as a photographer at the time.

His friend Lem Billings said, "I knew right away that Jackie was different from all the other girls Jack had been dating. She was more intelligent, more literary, more substantial."

Jackie was born on July 28, 1929. She grew up wealthy in New York City. She was sent to a private school, where one of her teachers wrote that she was "a darling child, the prettiest little girl; very clever; very artistic, and full of the devil." But her parents divorced when she was ten, and she became shy and reserved.

Though not rambunctious and spirited in the way of his sisters, Jackie had a lot in common with Jack. Just as he had, Jackie had spent a lot of time alone reading. She found comfort in books, much more than in people. Like Jack, she went to boarding school in high school. She was very smart and sophisticated, she spoke French fluently—and she was Catholic.

The two were married in Newport, Rhode Island, on September 12, 1953. It was a very large and fancy wedding. He was 36; she was 24.

"I married a whirlwind," Jackie said, referring to the hectic political life she entered. Although she was shy, she supported Jack's political ambitions. She learned how to campaign and how to talk with people she didn't know. She became one of Jack's greatest assets.

Not long after they were married, Jack could not stand the pain in his back anymore. He decided to have surgery on his spine, even though doctors warned that the operation could kill him.

It almost did. He got an infection, which his body couldn't fight because of the steroids he was taking. He went into a coma. Doctors were surprised when he survived. No person with Addison's disease had ever before lived through such major surgery.

But the operation was only partly successful. Doctors were not sure Jack would ever walk again. A few months later he had to have another operation to remove a steel plate they had put in his back and that was causing more infection.

Jack had to take time off from the Senate to recuperate from these operations. Instead of harming his career, as the Kennedys feared, it benefited him. The public could see how courageous he was. While he was recuperating, he worked on a book about the history of the Senate and about senators he admired. The trait he admired most was courage: the courage to do what you feel is right, even if it goes against what other people believe. The book, *Profiles in Courage,* explained his political philosophy. It was published in 1956.

There were 800 people at Jack and Jackie's wedding service, and 1,200 at the reception. People lined the streets outside the church to see the bride and groom.

That summer, at the Democratic National Convention, Adlai Stevenson was running for President, and Jack tried to get nominated as his Vice President. He lost out to a man named Estes Kefauver. Jack made a wonderful concession speech, which was broadcast on national television. Stevenson and Kefauver went on to lose the election to Dwight D. Eisenhower and Richard Nixon. But Jack's speech got him noticed all across the country.

Courage and Politics

"THE STORIES OF PAST COURAGE...CAN TEACH,
THEY CAN OFFER HOPE, THEY CAN PROVIDE INSPIRATION.
BUT THEY CANNOT SUPPLY COURAGE ITSELF.
FOR THIS EACH MAN MUST LOOK INTO HIS OWN SOUL."

PROFILES IN COURAGE, 1956

Jack didn't like the public to know he was in pain, but he often had trouble walking, bending over, and standing up. He could not hide his back surgeries, but they did not hurt his career—in fact, the public saw him for the courageous man he was. Here he signs copies of his Pulitzer Prize-winning book, which he wrote while recovering from back surgery. He once said that he would rather have the Pulitzer than the Presidency. So far he is the only person to get both!

The year 1957 was a great one for Jack. In January he won a seat on the Senate Foreign Relations Committee, one of the highest honors in the Senate. His book *Profiles in Courage* won the Pulitzer Prize for biography. And on November 27, the Kennedys' daughter, Caroline, was born.

Given his growing fame, he and his family talked about the Presidency. Could he win it? Was he ready? Was the country ready? The biggest obstacle was his religion. Although he had not been as religious a boy as his mother would have liked, he was a Catholic, and there was still great prejudice in the United States against Catholics. People worried that a Catholic President would be bad for the country because he would have to answer to the Pope, the leader of the Catholic Church. But Jack said that separation of church and state was in the U.S. Constitution. He would never do anything against the Constitution.

He knew that the only other Catholic to run for President, Al Smith, had lost to Herbert Hoover in a landslide in 1928. So Jack decided to test the waters. He started making speeches around the country. His brothers, Bobby and Teddy, helped him. Pictures of Jack and glamorous Jackie appeared on magazine covers. Things seemed to be going very well. On January 2, 1960, he announced his candidacy for the Presidency of the United States. He was only 42 years old.

Jack did very well in the primaries and soon became his party's front-runner. In July 1960, he headed to the Democratic National Convention in Los Angeles with high hopes. In fact, "High Hopes" was one of his campaign songs. In the original "High Hopes," Frank Sinatra sang about an optimistic ant who could move a rubber tree plant. Now Sinatra sang for his favorite candidate:

Everyone is voting for Jack.
'Cause he's got what all the rest lack.
Everyone wants to back Jack.
Jack is on the right track.
'Cause he's got High Hopes!
He's got High Hopes!
1960's the year for his High Hopes!

In July 1960, Jack Kennedy headed for the Democratic National Convention with a strong lead and high hopes. But it was not a sure thing he would win his party's nomination for President.

But many people, including some party leaders, felt that Jack was too young to be President. Former Democratic President Harry S. Truman made it clear in a speech that Jack should wait his turn.

Jack made a speech back, saying that he was ready, that he had won the primaries, and that he would win the Presidency. What Truman and the public did not know was that Jack never thought he would live a long life because of all his illnesses. For Jack there was no such thing as waiting his turn.

Jack won the nomination on the first ballot. He surprised many people by choosing his chief rival, Lyndon Baines Johnson, to be his vice presidential candidate. LBJ was a good choice; he was an experienced and well-known senator. As a Texan, he would bring in a lot of electoral college votes from his home state and help win more votes from the rest of the South than Kennedy would get without him.

Kennedy and Johnson ran against Richard Nixon and his running mate, Henry Cabot Lodge, Jr. Nixon had been Vice President for eight years under the very popular Dwight D. Eisenhower. Lodge was Kennedy's old Senate rival, the one he'd defeated back in 1952. Lodge was well known nationwide and was the U.S. delegate to the United Nations. They were a formidable team to beat.

Walter Cronkite, the famous television news anchorman, interviewed the two presidential candidates as the campaign began. Nixon was relaxed, friendly, and at ease. Jack, on the other hand, was nervous. He misspoke and looked uncomfortable. He came off badly. Jack learned from that experience. He practiced and got much better at being on television.

On September 26, 1960, 70 million Americans turned on their televisions to watch the first ever televised presidential debate. Jack had been campaigning in California and looked tanned, handsome, and relaxed. He had rested, and his back was not hurting very much. Nixon later wrote, "I had never seen him looking so fit." Jack was a handsome man, more than six feet tall, with a full head of reddish brown hair and greenish gray eyes. And thanks to Jackie's flair for fashion, he dressed well.

Nixon was not handsome. Compared with Jack he was homely. When he showed up at the debate, he was 20 pounds underweight and looked pale and haggard. He had hurt his knee in August and had spent two weeks in the hospital. His shirt didn't fit, and he had refused the TV station's offer of more makeup

The 1960 presidential campaign was the first to be won— and lost—on television.

to cover up the "five o'clock shadow" left by the stubble of his beard. Under the hot studio lights, Nixon sweated a lot; Kennedy did not.

Both men were very smart and gave good answers. People who listened to the debate on the radio thought that Nixon had won. But more people watched the debate on TV—and they declared Kennedy the winner hands down. His answers were smooth, his smile wide and bright, and he had "charisma."

Charisma was a word people used for Kennedy wherever he went. He had a self-confidence, an almost magical self-assurance about him. And although he was only four years younger than Nixon, Jack seemed much younger and much more vigorous. He used that in his campaign. Nixon and his supporters argued that Nixon had much more experience. Kennedy and his team said the country needed a new, younger leadership. Jack talked about helping people: hungry children, farmers, the elderly, and African Americans. He talked about medical care and about the race for the moon and outer space. He called for a new, vigorous America: a New Frontier.

The most serious issue in the campaign was the threat of nuclear war. At the time, the United States was in what was called the Cold War with the U.S.S.R., or Soviet Union. The Soviet Union was a large country made up of 15 republics, the largest of which was Russia. It was a Communist dictatorship. Soviet leaders restricted the way their citizens practiced religion and severely punished people who spoke out against the government. Like the United States, it was a "superpower," with a strong military and many nuclear weapons.

Jack talks to a poor family in rural West Virginia during his campaign for the Presidency. Even though he grew up wealthy, he understood the problems and needs of people who did not have enough money, and he wanted very much to help them.

Chief Justice Earl Warren swore in John F. Kennedy as President, and Marian Anderson, the famous African-American contralto, sang the national anthem. Poet Robert Frost read a poem he had written especially for the occasion. But Frost had trouble finishing it because the sun was in his eyes, so he recited "The Gift Outright," a poem he had written 20 years before.

Since the end of World War II, distrust and suspicion between the two superpowers had been growing. This led to a race to make and stockpile nuclear weapons. In 1960 it seemed certain that it would be up to the next President of the United States not only to prevent the Soviet Union from taking over more countries, but also to save the world from nuclear destruction.

Nixon said that because of his eight years of experience as Vice President, he would be the better man to deal with the Soviet Union. But Kennedy said the Soviets were "winning" the Cold War because the Republicans had not done a good enough job of dealing with them.

On election night 1960, Jack and his whole family waited for the results in Hyannis Port, where the extended Kennedy family now had many houses. As the returns came in from the East Coast, the Kennedys' favorite word, "terrific," could be heard all over the Kennedy compound. But as the night wore on and votes started coming in from the West, it didn't look so good for their boy. Richard Nixon, who was from California—the most populous state in the nation—was getting more and more votes. It looked as though Nixon would win.

Jack went to bed not knowing if he had won or lost. In the morning he was awakened by his little daughter Caroline. She jumped on his bed shouting, "Good morning, Mr. President!" John F. Kennedy was the youngest person ever elected President. He would be the 35th President of the United States, the first one born in the 20th century. But the vote was very close. He would have to prove himself.

On Inauguration Day, January 20, 1961, some 150 people were seated on the platform; 16 of these were Kennedys. His mother proudly said, "Of all the millions of women in the world, to think I was the one. That I was the mother. It was just overwhelming." She marveled at how strong his voice sounded on such a cold day.

John F. Kennedy, or JFK, as he came to be known, gave one of the most famous speeches of his life. He talked about the threat of nuclear war and of the need to be strong against our enemies. He spoke of poverty around the world and of our responsibility to help others. Just as his parents had told him growing up, Kennedy told all Americans: Do something in public service. Make a contribution to your country and the world.

One of the first things the new President did was sign an executive order on March 1, 1961, establishing the Peace Corps. Based on a bill Senator Hubert Humphrey had introduced in the Senate in 1960, the Peace Corps would use volunteers to work with people in underdeveloped countries to help improve their lives. President Kennedy said, "Men and women will be expected to work and live alongside the nationals of the country in which they are stationed—doing the same work, eating the same food, talking the same language." Three days later he appointed his sister Eunice's husband, Sargent Shriver, to be the organization's director. In August the first group of volunteers landed in Africa at the airport in Accra, Ghana. To the delight of the waiting crowd, they sang the Ghanian national anthem in Twi, the local language. That September Congress formally authorized the Peace Corps.

"AND SO, MY FELLOW AMERICANS: ASK NOT WHAT YOUR COUNTRY CAN DO FOR YOU— ASK WHAT YOU CAN DO FOR YOUR COUNTRY."

These words from Kennedy's Inaugural Address became his most famous statement. They symbolized his spirit of service, of hope, and his belief that every person can make a difference.

Jackie Kennedy preferred to keep her children's lives private, but Jack encouraged photographers to take pictures of them. These pictures—Caroline on her pony, Macaroni, and John Jr. peeking out from his father's desk—are two of the most famous.

It seemed as if the whole world fell in love with Jack and his glamorous wife. Women started copying the way Jackie dressed. They watched the way she decorated the White House and invited famous musicians to perform there. And everyone fell in love with little Caroline and the new baby. Jackie had been pregnant when Jack won the election. Two weeks later, on November 25, 1960, their son, John F. Kennedy, Jr., was born.

The President loved to have his children visit him in the Oval Office. And he loved when the press told "Caroline stories." Once, when asked a question about her daddy's work, Caroline said, "He's not doing anything. He's just sitting up there with his shoes and socks off doing nothing." Then there was the hamster incident. Caroline's hamsters, Debbie and Billy, kept getting out of their cages. The President found them under his bed and in his bathroom. Reporters battered Press Secretary Pierre Salinger with questions: Had a security officer been assigned to them?

"WE STAND TODAY ON THE EDGE
OF A NEW FRONTIER—
THE FRONTIER OF THE 1960s—
A FRONTIER OF UNKNOWN
OPPORTUNITIES AND PERILS—
A FRONTIER OF UNFULFILLED
HOPES AND THREATS."

Had Caroline helped them escape? Salinger assured them that "stern measures have been taken to confine them to quarters." Reporters had fun with this kind of story, in part because the real news was scary. President Kennedy said he was surprised to find, once he entered the Oval Office, that things were as bad as he had claimed while he was campaigning.

In April 1961, just three months after he took office, President Kennedy had to deal with Cuba. Cuba is a small island country just 90 miles to the south of Florida, run by a dictator named Fidel Castro. At that time Castro was aligned with the Communist Soviet Union and its head, Nikita Khrushchev. Many Americans felt it would be much safer for the United States if Castro were taken out of power. So President Kennedy approved a plan that had been hatched by the Eisenhower Administration. The United States would help Cuban rebels living in the United States invade Cuba at the Bay of Pigs and overthrow Castro. Military advisers and the CIA assured President Kennedy that the plan would work.

The plan did not work. The invasion was a total failure. Castro's soldiers killed or captured all 1,500 rebel invaders. The "Bay of Pigs," as the incident became known, was a huge embarrassment for the President, his administration, and the United States.

President Kennedy was upset and angry. Publicly he accepted responsibility for the failure. At a press conference he told reporters, "There is an old saying that victory has a hundred fathers and defeat is an orphan...."

Privately he swore that he would learn from his mistake. He met with former President Eisenhower, who chewed him out. The former Commander in Chief told him that as President he should always know everything that is going on in a military operation, that he should ask lots of questions, and that he should surround himself with people he trusted.

Jack already had one trusted adviser: his brother Bobby. Soon after he had been elected, he had followed his father's advice and appointed Bobby attorney general, the chief law officer of the country. Jack worried that

Two brothers. Bobby, left, was Jack's best man at his wedding and his closest confidant during his Presidency. Bobby later went on to be a senator and a champion of civil rights. He ran for President in 1968 but was assassinated during his campaign.

people would think he was playing favorites by appointing his brother to such a high position. But after the Bay of Pigs, Jack knew how important trust was. From then on he depended on his own judgment and on the advice of close advisers, especially Bobby.

Six weeks after the Bay of Pigs, President Kennedy faced his main enemy head-on. He met with Soviet Premier Nikita Khrushchev at a summit in Vienna, Austria, in June 1961.

Kennedy's main goal in going to the summit was to convince Khrushchev that the two superpowers had to avoid nuclear war. He gave the Soviet leader a model of Old Ironsides, a historic U.S. battleship

During President and Mrs. Kennedy's first official visit to France in June 1961, they were the guests of French President and Mrs. Charles de Gaulle (below, on either side of JFK) at the Theater of Versailles. Jackie, who spoke French, was such a hit with the people that Jack jokingly identified himself as "the man who accompanied Jackie Kennedy to Paris."

Things were so tense at the Vienna summit that when a photographer asked Khrushchev (to the right of JFK) and Kennedy to shake hands for a picture, the Soviet leader pointed at Jackie and said, "I'd rather shake hands with her."

docked in Boston Harbor. He told Khrushchev that back in 1812, when it fought, the ship's guns could fire only a half mile. In those days, countries could recover from wars in months. But with nuclear weapons that can fire great distances and blow up huge areas, the whole world could be destroyed. "We can't let that happen," he said.

He also wanted to make sure Khrushchev would leave West Berlin alone. West Berlin was a free city in the middle of Soviet-controlled East Germany. Even the other half of the city, East Berlin, was under Soviet control.

Khrushchev barely let Kennedy talk. He lectured him on the Soviet Union's right to exist and to spread Soviet political ideas all over the world.

In August 1961, East German police began building a wall of stone and barbed wire to keep East Germans from fleeing to West Berlin and freedom from Communism. Some East Germans still escaped after the wall was built. In June 1963 JFK traveled to Berlin to show his support for the people there. He said, "All free men, wherever they may live, are citizens of Berlin, and, therefore, as a free man, I take pride in the words 'Ich bin ein Berliner.'"

He threatened war and acted like a bully. Khrushchev was older and a much more experienced politician. Jack felt young and off balance. Plus, his back hurt him badly during the summit. Every few hours he had to have an injection for pain.

When he got home, President Kennedy felt terrible about his performance at the summit. He knew he had let the Soviet leader beat him. He also knew that for the sake of the United States and the whole world, he couldn't let Khrushchev go on thinking that he was weak. To avoid war, he had to convince the Soviet Union that the U.S. was willing to fight.

Over the next few months, he readied American forces for war. Khrushchev backed down. He did not take over West Berlin. But he did build a wall separating East and West Berlin. Neither man had "won," exactly, but Jack showed Khrushchev he couldn't be bullied.

Meanwhile, on the home front, President Kennedy was trying to enact his New Frontier programs. He wasn't able to get Congress to do as much as he wanted, but he was successful in some areas, such as getting aid to the poor and raising the minimum hourly wage. He beefed up the space program and issued the challenge for the United States to put a man on the moon before the end of the decade.

JFK was well liked and had a very high popularity rating both at home and abroad. He was charming and funny. At press conferences he had a way of taking a tough question, making a joke, and then answering it so that the person who asked it went from being angry to laughing and nodding in agreement.

But an area that gave him trouble was civil rights. It was a terrible time for African Americans in the segregated South. They were being

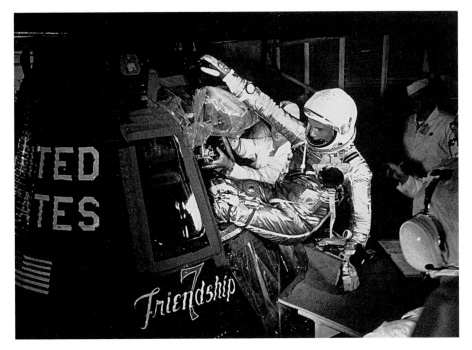

On February 20, 1962, Astronaut John Glenn entered his spacecraft (left) to become the first American to orbit the Earth. This Marine Corps Astronaut Insignia (right) was given to him to commemorate that flight.

denied their constitutional right to vote and were forced to go to inferior, segregated schools. They also were not allowed to eat, live, or go to movies wherever they chose.

President Kennedy cared about helping African-American people. He appointed Thurgood Marshall, an African-American civil rights lawyer, to the U.S. Court of Appeals for the Second Circuit, a powerful position. But civil rights leaders thought Kennedy wasn't doing enough. He was in a tough spot. Jack knew that if he came out too much in favor of civil rights, powerful southern congressmen would block his New Frontier programs. And he would lose the votes of white Southerners in the next presidential election. But in October 1962, his hand was forced. An African-American man named James Meredith tried to enroll in the University of Mississippi. Thousands of white people rioted to protest his enrollment. President Kennedy ordered 30,000 Army and National Guard soldiers to keep order and to make sure that Meredith and other African Americans were given their constitutional right to attend "Ole Miss." The battle lasted 14 hours. Hundreds of people were hurt; two were killed. In the end, Meredith, protected by some National Guard soldiers, was able to attend the university. Ole Miss was finally integrated.

That same month, President Kennedy had to face another crisis with Cuba. This one could have ended the world. U.S. spy planes taking photographs of Cuba discovered that the Soviet Union was building facilities to house nuclear missiles on the island. Missiles fired from Cuba would easily reach the United States. The President had to stop the Soviets— without starting a nuclear war.

Kennedy's military advisers told him to invade Cuba. They said that there were no nuclear weapons in Cuba yet. Now would be the time to attack. But the President had learned from his mistakes at the Bay of Pigs. He was cautious. Instead of attacking, he went on national television and told the American people about the missiles. He ordered U.S. Navy ships to blockade Cuba. To prevent weapons from reaching the island, Soviet ships would be ordered to turn around. But would the ships turn around, or would they start a war?

President Kennedy secretly negotiated with Nikita Khrushchev.

In the spring of 1963, unarmed African Americans in Birmingham, Alabama, peacefully protested against segregation. But white authorities attacked them with fire hoses and dogs. In June President Kennedy introduced a major civil rights bill into Congress. And in August Martin Luther King, Jr. led thousands on a march on Washington and gave his famous "I Have a Dream" speech. JFK didn't join the march, but he gave his approval.

He promised him that the United States would not invade Cuba if the Soviets would not put missiles there.

It was a terrifying and dangerous 13 days. People around the U.S. placed food, water, and other necessities for survival in underground bomb shelters. At the last possible moment, the Soviet ships turned around. Khrushchev promised not to put nuclear missiles on Cuba. In return, President Kennedy promised to take away some missiles the U.S. had put in Turkey near the Soviet border.

Many years later we found out what President Kennedy did not know: The Soviets already had nuclear missiles in Cuba. If we had invaded, they could very well have used the missiles against us. By negotiating instead of attacking, President Kennedy had saved the world from nuclear war.

President Kennedy knew the world had come way too close to destruction. In June 1963 he gave what many people call "the speech of his life." The talk, at American University, called for world peace. He said, "I am talking about genuine peace, the kind of peace that makes life on earth worth living, the kind that enables men and nations to grow and to hope and to build a better life for their children—not merely peace for Americans but peace for all men and women—not merely peace in our time but peace for all time." President Kennedy insisted on working for better relations with the Soviet Union. "For peace is a process—a way of solving problems," he said.

This speech was the beginning of détente—the easing of tensions between the two superpowers. It led to the Nuclear Test Ban Treaty, which was signed by the United States, the Soviet Union, and Great Britain in October 1963. This treaty prohibited the testing of nuclear weapons in the atmosphere, in outer space, or underwater. Kennedy and Khrushchev also established a hotline between the White House and the Kremlin so they could communicate with each other immediately and avoid nuclear war.

Americans and people around the world had confidence in President Kennedy and real hope for world peace.

In August 1963 the Kennedys suffered a personal loss. Jackie prematurely gave birth to a son, Patrick Bouvier Kennedy, who died two days later. The President and First Lady were devastated.

But they had to look ahead. The next presidential election would be in November 1964, and the President and his staff were starting to think about the campaign. So were Republican challengers. President Kennedy had high hopes for a second term in office. He wanted to make more progress toward a lasting peace with the Soviet Union. He especially hoped to accomplish more at home. He wanted to combat poverty, create more jobs, and put an end to racial injustice.

LIFE

THE DANGER-FILLED WEEK OF DECISION

CUBA

CUBA'S MISSILE RANGE

IN BRIE

The Grea

San Francisco
2,565 miles

UNITED STATES

Washington, D.C.
1,128 miles

CUBA

Range of SS-4 medium-range ballistic missile: 1,200 miles

Range of SS-5 intermediate-range ballistic missile: 2,500 miles

Cuba is so close to the U.S. that nuclear missiles fired from that country could reach the U.S. in a few hours. Schoolchildren all over the country practiced how to "duck and cover" in case of a nuclear strike.

U.S. NAVY OFF CUBA

Mr. PABLO CASALS, *Cello*

Mr. Mieczyslaw Horszowski, *Piano*

Mr. Alexander Schneider, *Violin*

Monday, November 13, 1961
THE WHITE HOUSE

The Kennedys invited many musicians, painters, writers, and other artists to the White House. The President felt that the arts should be an important part of a nation's purpose. Here Pablo Casals, then the world's most famous cellist, greets President and Mrs. Kennedy and their guests after a performance. Jack's mother, Rose, is in white, at the end of the first row.

But he knew to get reelected he had to keep the voters in the South happy. That's why, in November 1963, he and Jackie set off for Texas. The First Lady didn't usually go on trips with her husband, but since Patrick's death, they had been spending more time together. They seemed closer than they had been since the early days of their marriage.

Some of their friends advised them not to go to Texas; they said that too many people in Texas—white people—were angry at the President because he was in favor of civil rights. But that is precisely why he felt he needed to go: He wanted to mend political fences so he could be assured reelection. Although he was very popular in most of the country, he knew enough about politics to know he had to work hard to stay popular.

On November 22, 1963, the President spoke at a breakfast meeting in Fort Worth, Texas. Shortly after 11:30 a.m., President and Mrs. Kennedy landed at Love Field, in nearby Dallas. They greeted the waiting crowd, shaking hands, waving, smiling broadly. Later, watching the film of Jack and Jackie at Love Field, what would strike everyone was how happy, young, and alive they both looked.

President and Mrs. Kennedy got into an open limousine with Texas Governor John Connally and his wife. They were part of a motorcade traveling to the Dallas Trade Mart, where the President would be speaking at a luncheon. Three cars back were Vice President and Mrs. Johnson.

People gathered at the Dallas airport and lined the city streets to see President Kennedy in person. It was the largest crowd ever to greet a visitor in Dallas. He insisted on riding in an open car, which added an extra challenge for the Secret Service agents and local police protecting him.

There is a famous picture of him smiling at the crowd just before—

A noise like a firecracker. A gun. The bullet hit President Kennedy in the neck. A second shot hit him in the back of his head. That bullet killed him. Jack was wearing a back brace that kept him upright. If he hadn't been wearing the brace, would he have slumped? Would the second, fatal shot have missed him?

Jackie said later, "I kept thinking, if I hadn't been looking left, if I had been looking right, I would have seen the first shot hit him, and I would have pulled him down, so the second shot wouldn't hit him."

This is President Kennedy just moments before he was shot. At the time half of his Cabinet, including Press Secretary Pierre Salinger and Secretary of State Dean Rusk, was on a plane to Japan. When they heard the news, they ordered the plane to return to Washington.

November 22, 1963. To the people who were alive at the time, it is a date like September 11, 2001, when terrorists flew passenger planes into the twin towers of New York's World Trade Center, the Pentagon in Washington, D.C., and a field in Pennsylvania, killing almost 4,000 people; or for an earlier generation, December 7, 1941, when the Japanese attacked Pearl Harbor in Hawaii. They can remember exactly where they were when they heard the news that President Kennedy had been shot.

The first bulletin interrupted the CBS soap opera *As the World Turns.* Two characters were talking about the marital problems of "Bob" when

"WE HAVE SUFFERED A LOSS THAT CANNOT BE WEIGHED....I WILL DO MY BEST. THAT IS ALL I CAN DO. I ASK FOR YOUR HELP—AND GOD'S."

—LYNDON BAINES JOHNSON

Vice President Johnson is sworn in as President by Judge Sarah Hughes, a federal judge from Dallas. They are on Air Force One, the President's plane, as it is preparing for takeoff from Love Field. Johnson's wife, Lady Bird, and Mrs. Kennedy are by his side. President Kennedy's casket is also on the plane. This was the only time Jackie left her husband's body that whole day.

the screen suddenly went black. The words "CBS News Bulletin" appeared in white letters, then anchorman Walter Cronkite's voice came on: "In Dallas, Texas, three shots were fired at President Kennedy's motorcade. The first reports say the President was seriously wounded...." Governor Connally had been shot, too. President Kennedy was rushed to the hospital. But he never had a chance of surviving.

At 2:38 p.m., Walter Cronkite, fighting back tears, made the announcement from the CBS studio in New York: "The President died at two o'clock eastern standard time....The President is dead...." Cameras panned to people hearing the news in New York's Times Square and all over the country. Everywhere, people were crying.

For the next three and a half days, 18 million viewers stayed glued to their televisions. There were no commercials, no other programs, just as on the days after September 11, 2001. People all over the world, even in the Soviet Union, stared at the screen, hungry for any new detail.

They soon found out that a man had fired a rifle from a window on the sixth floor of the Texas School Book Depository, a company that fulfilled school book orders. Police arrested Lee Harvey Oswald about an hour and a half after the President was killed. He was in a movie theater. The rifle police recovered had his palm print on it, and they were able to trace the gun to Oswald through the mail-order firm he had bought it from. Police also learned that he was pro-Castro and had a Russian wife. In jail, Oswald claimed he was innocent, that he did not kill the President.

But President Kennedy was dead.

The country needed a President right away. Vice President Lyndon Johnson was sworn in as President on Air Force One before it left Texas.

Back in Massachusetts, the Kennedy family gathered together. Rose and Teddy told Joseph, who was very old and sick. One can only imagine how he felt, losing a third child, his second son, the one who had fulfilled his dream by becoming President.

In Washington, Jackie planned the funeral, modeling it after Abraham Lincoln's. She stayed calm though grief-stricken. Her dignity and poise gave the nation something to hold on to. So did the new President, who seemed sad but in control.

Evening papers rushed to print the news of the President's assassination. People grabbed papers as soon as they were available. Here, commuters search for details about the tragedy.

KENNEDY EXTRA

PRESIDENT DEA

Shot by Assassin

American 7

Highlights of Kennedy's Career

On November 24, President Kennedy's closed casket was on view in the Capitol Rotunda. People watched on television as thousands of mourners filed by. Suddenly, more horror unfolded before their eyes.

Lee Harvey Oswald was being led from the Dallas City Jail to an armored truck, when all of a sudden someone shouted, "He's been shot!" Some TV stations were covering Oswald so their viewers saw it live; other channels broke away from the Capitol Rotunda to Dallas. Jack Ruby, a nightclub owner, had murdered Oswald. The chief suspect was dead. He could never be interrogated.

To this day there are questions about the assassination. Did Lee Harvey Oswald act alone or was he part of a conspiracy? Was he the only one who shot the President? Why did Jack Ruby kill him? The Warren Commission, appointed by President Johnson to investigate the assassination, concluded that Oswald had acted alone. But people still argue about who killed JFK.

Hopes were dashed that November day. Hopes of a man; hopes of a family; hopes of a nation; hopes of a world.

John Fitzgerald Kennedy died at age 46. No one knows what he would have accomplished if he had won a second term. Would he have gone down in history as a great President? He certainly seemed to be heading that way.

For many people Jack became perfect in his death. He became more of a myth than a man. In some ways, the myth is as important as the man himself. John F. Kennedy symbolizes strength, vigor, wisdom, and caring for others. He symbolizes determination. And high hopes.

John Jr. (above) would later say he had no memory of his father. But this picture of him saluting the President's casket has become a symbol of the tenacity of the Kennedy spirit. It was John's third birthday.

Mourners line the Memorial Bridge in Washington, D.C., as a horse-drawn carriage carrying Kennedy's flag-draped casket makes its way to Arlington National Cemetery.

"LET THE WORD GO FORTH FROM THIS TIME AND PLACE,
TO FRIEND AND FOE ALIKE, THAT THE TORCH HAS
BEEN PASSED TO A NEW GENERATION OF AMERICANS—
BORN IN THIS CENTURY, TEMPERED BY WAR,
DISCIPLINED BY A HARD AND BITTER PEACE..."

JOHN FITZGERALD KENNEDY
1917 — 1963

AFTERWORD

President John Fitzgerald Kennedy was buried at Arlington National Cemetery on November 25, 1963. Jackie lit an eternal flame at his grave (opposite). If rain or snow or wind puts it out, a spark ignites to light it again immediately. So JFK's flame is always burning.

President Lyndon Johnson was able to get many of President Kennedy's programs passed in Congress. Civil rights legislation passed, as did legislation to help the poor.

Jack's sisters and brothers, children, and nieces and nephews went on to serve the country in different ways, including politics, public service, writing, and charitable works. Members of the Kennedy family, inspired by Rosemary, started the Special Olympics. Bobby Kennedy was elected to the U.S. Senate from New York and ran for President in 1968. During the campaign, he, too, was assassinated. The youngest of Jack's brothers, Edward (Teddy), has been a powerful and important Democratic senator representing Massachusetts for 40 years. He has championed the cause of the poor and the needy.

Jackie died of cancer in 1994. She was laid to rest next to President Kennedy. Both Caroline and John Jr. graduated from law school. John founded a political magazine called *George.* He was killed in 1999 when the plane he was flying crashed off the coast of Cape Cod. Caroline is an author and is very involved in Kennedy Library programs and in public service. She is married and has three children: Rose, Tatiana, and John.

The Peace Corps is still active, as is the space program. There are buildings, airports, streets, and schools around the globe named for John F. Kennedy. His ideas, his words, and his hopes for peace and a better life endure.

Jack never thought he would live a long life. But he hoped to inspire others to give to the world. It was his firm belief that children, like you, are "the world's most valuable resource and its best hope for the future."

CHRONOLOGY

1917 John Fitzgerald Kennedy is born in Brookline, Massachusetts, on May 29.

1919 Jack becomes very ill with scarlet fever and almost dies.

1927 Kennedy family moves to New York but still spends summers in Massachusetts, at Hyannis Port on Cape Cod.

1930 Jack goes off to the Canterbury School in New Milford, Connecticut.

1931 Transfers to Choate Academy in Wallingford, Connecticut, for high school.

1935 Graduates from Choate and is voted most likely to succeed; breaking with family tradition, Jack enrolls at Princeton University but has to leave due to illness.

1936 Enrolls at Harvard University, as his father and Joe Jr. had done.

1938–39 Spends summer in Europe; writes his senior thesis on why England was slow to stop Hitler.

1940 Graduates from Harvard with honors; publishes thesis as the book *Why England Slept.*

1941 Joins the Navy.

1943 Jack's boat, PT 109, is rammed into and cut in half by a Japanese destroyer on August 2; saves the ten other survivors; finally rescued on August 8.

1944 Joseph Kennedy, Jr., dies in plane explosion over the English Channel while on a secret wartime mission.

1946 Jack runs for U.S. House of Representatives and wins.

1947 Starts serving the first of three consecutive two-year terms in Congress; diagnosed with Addison's disease.

1948 Sister Kathleen (Kick) dies in a plane crash.

1952 Runs for Senate and wins.

1953 Marries Jacqueline Bouvier in Newport, Rhode Island, on September 12.

1954–5 Has series of operations on his back; writes *Profiles in Courage,* which is published in 1956.

1957 *Profiles in Courage* wins Pulitzer Prize; daughter Caroline is born on November 27.

1960

January 2 Announces his candidacy for the Presidency of the United States.

July 15 Accepts the nomination of the Democratic Party and picks Lyndon Baines Johnson to be his running mate.

September 26 Debates Richard Nixon in the first of four televised debates.

November 8 Elected President.

November 25 John Jr. is born.

1961

January 20 John F. Kennedy is inaugurated as the 35th President of the United States.

In March Announces the formation of the Peace Corps.

In April Tries to help Cuban rebels overthrow Fidel Castro; failure becomes known as the "Bay of Pigs."

In May Makes speech asking Congress for more money for the space program and declares his goal of "landing a man on the moon and returning him safely to Earth."

In June Meets with Soviet Premier Nikita Khrushchev in Vienna, Austria; war avoided but Soviets build a wall separating East and West Berlin.

1962

In October African American James Meredith tries to enroll in the University of Mississippi; race riots ensue and President Kennedy calls in Army and National Guard; university is integrated.

Also in October The U.S. finds out the Soviet Union is putting nuclear missiles in Cuba; for 13 days the world stands on the brink of nuclear war; JFK peacefully forces the Soviets to back down, ending the Cuban missile crisis and avoiding nuclear war.

1963

June 10 President Kennedy gives a speech at American University that begins détente—the easing of tensions between the U.S. and the Soviet Union.

Also in June JFK sends a major civil rights bill to Congress.

August 7 Son Patrick Bouvier is born prematurely and dies two days later.

November 22 President Kennedy is shot and killed in Dallas, Texas, allegedly by Lee Harvey Oswald.

November 25 President Kennedy is buried on John Jr.'s third birthday.

RESOURCES

There is a wealth of information about President Kennedy. These are the resources I found most helpful.

BOOKS

An asterisk (*) indicates a book especially for young people.

Ballard, Robert D. with Michael Hamilton Morgan. *Collision With History: The Search for John F. Kennedy's PT 109.* Washington, DC: National Geographic Society, 2002.

*****Collier, Christopher, and James Lincoln Collier.** *The United States in the Cold War, 1945–1989.* New York: Benchmark Books/Marshall Cavendish, 2002.

Goodwin, Doris Kearns. *The Fitzgeralds and the Kennedys: An American Saga.* New York: Simon & Schuster, 1987.

*****Harper, Judith E.** *John F. Kennedy: Our Thirty-Fifth President.* Chanhassen, MN: The Child's World, 2002.

Kennedy, John F. *Profiles in Courage.* There are many editions of this book. I used the one I had as a child, the Teen Age Abridged Edition, published by Scholastic, 1964.

Reeves, Richard. *President Kennedy: Profile of Power.* New York: Simon & Schuster, 1993.

Salinger, Pierre. *John F. Kennedy, Commander in Chief A Profile in Leadership.* New York: Penguin Studio, 1997.

MAGAZINES

"A Family Man With A Big New Job To Do," *LIFE,* November 21, 1960.

"America's Long Vigil: A permanent record of what we watched on television from November 22 to 25, 1963." *TV Guide,* January 25, 1964.

Dallek, Robert, "The Medical Ordeals of JFK," *Atlantic Monthly,* December 2002.

Miller, Llewellyn "The Delightful World of Caroline Kennedy," *Redbook,* June 1961.

The complete issues of the following magazines were devoted to JFK.

LIFE, November 29, 1963.

LIFE, December 6, 1963.

LIFE, Memorial Edition, 1963.

Look, November 17, 1964.

NEWSPAPERS

The *New York Times* on line has many articles about JFK. *(See Web site column at right.)*

Evening Chronicle, Allentown, PA, November 22, 1963.

VIDEOS

"Image of an Assassination: A New Look at the Zapruder Film," MPI Teleproductions; Authorized by the LMH Company, 1998.

"JFK Remembered" Starring Peter Jennings, Vestron, 1988.

"John Fitzgerald Kennedy: A Celebration of His Life and Times," Readers Digest Video, three volumes, 1998.

"Life in Camelot: The Kennedy Years," Kunhardt Productions, Inc., 1988.

"The Secret Service, Volume 3: JFK to Watergate, The Inside Story," The History Channel, 1995.

"The Speeches of John F. Kennedy," MPI Home Video, 1990.

"Thirteen Days," New Line Home Entertainment, 2001. (Although this is historical fiction about the Cuban missile crisis, it is based on a memoir of an associate of JFK's.)

"Walter Cronkite Remembers the 20th Century: Television, Politics & JFK," Readers Digest Association, Inc. in association with CBS, Inc. and Cronkite, Ward and Company, 1997.

WEB SITES

The American President
americanpresident.org

Arlington National Cemetery
arlingtoncemetery.com

JFK Link Speeches of JFK
jfklink.com

John F. Kennedy Library and Museum
www.cs.umb.edu/jfklibrary

The John F. Kennedy National Historical Site
nps.gov/jofi

The Museum of Broadcast Communications
museum.tv/index.shtml

National Geographic Society
nationalgeographic.com/pt109
(Go here for more about PT 109)

Naval Historical Center
history.navy.mil

The *New York Times*
nytimes.com

The Peace Corps
peacecorps.gov

The Sixth Floor Museum at Dealey Plaza
jfk.org

U.S. National Archives and Records Administration
archives.gov

United States Secret Service
ustreas.gov/usss/history.shtml

The White House
whitehouse.gov

INDEX

One of the world's largest nonprofit scientific and educational organizations, the National Geographic Society was founded in 1888 "for the increase and diffusion of geographic knowledge." Fulfilling this mission, the Society educates and inspires millions every day through its magazines, books, television programs, videos, maps and atlases, research grants, the National Geographic Bee, teacher workshops, and innovative classroom materials. The Society is supported through membership dues, charitable gifts, and income from the sale of its educational products. This support is vital to National Geographic's mission to increase global understanding and promote conservation of our planet through exploration, research, and education. For more information, please call 1-800-NGS LINE (647-5463) or write to the following address:

National Geographic Society, 1145 17th Street N.W. Washington, D.C. 20036-4688 U.S.A.

Visit the Society's Web site: **www.nationalgeographic.com**